Learning Floor Gymnastics at Home

Sebastian Gröning

The book:

From an early age, children are fascinated by defying gravity. Once they start walking, rolling movements catch their interest, and by the time they reach elementary school, they are eager to balance on their hands.

This book serves as a comprehensive guide to the essential floor gymnastics techniques taught in apparatus gymnastics, artistic gymnastics, and sports acrobatics. It includes preparatory exercises that can be performed at home with minimal equipment, making it a perfect supplement to club training or even a substitute for it.

To enhance the training process, the book also describes the most common spotting techniques for each exercise, allowing parents, relatives, and friends to actively participate in the practice sessions.

The Author:

Sebastian Gröning grew up in the small German state of Saarland. At the age of 28, he began his career as a sports acrobat, and after two years, he also started working as a coach in the club sector. Alongside this, he practiced acrobatics at home, in parks - wherever life took him.

After moving to Lower Austria, he started his own acrobatics groups. Since he has enjoyed writing since he was fourteen, the idea of sharing his knowledge in book form began to take shape.

Learning Floor Gymnastics at Home

from

Sebastian Gröning

Amazon KDP

1. Edition, 2024

© 2024 Sebastian Gröning all rights reserved.

cover design: hollybookstore

Illustrations: chathuri_suga, Dulnethu, Yvren

Translation: ChatGPT, Sebastian Gröning

Post edit: Sebastian Gröning

ISBN: 9798335979849

Independent published

Owner, Editor, Author:

Sebastian Gröning

Götzwiesenstraße 8, 3032 Eichgraben, Österreich

sagroening@gmx.at

Inhaltsverzeichnis

Foreword

Nearly every child comes in contact with floor gymnastics sooner or later. In playgroups, they are attempting their first somersaults, trying out cartwheel techniques, and eventually, all kids make some attempt to stand on their heads or to turn everything upside down.

At school, I constantly see children doing cartwheels during breaks in such amounts that just watching them makes my muscles feel sore. For some, this journey continues in sports clubs where these fundamental techniques are perfected and advanced ones are taught.

Others learn to use their mattresses, couches, and other household items as training equipment. I've worked with many gymnasts who taught themselves how to do a back handspring at home.

Garden trampolines, airtracks, and trampoline parks further expand the possibilities for improving floor gymnastics skills outside of organized sports.

This book is for:

Anyone interested in getting started with floor gymnastics.
Fitness enthusiasts looking for clear instructions on how to improve their skills.
Parents who want to support and guide their children on their gymnastics journey.

It provides an overview of techniques that can be safely practiced alone, as well as guidance on how to securely learn more complex gymnastics skills.

However, even the best book cannot always replace personal training. I generally recommend supplementing home training with opportunities to learn under professional supervision in a gymnastics club or similar setting, if available.

Especially complex techniques require a lot of patience and, for some gymnasts, extensive material and safety measures that are difficult to replicate at home.

I hope you enjoy learning and practicing the techniques shown here. The exercises are organized by difficulty and sometimes by methodological progression. Therefore, I recommend going through them in order and not working through the book from back to front in a rush.

What is Floor Gymastics

Floor gymnastics has a long tradition among jugglers and circus performers, who have been captivating audiences with it since ancient times. The first regulated forms appeared in Germany with the so-called „free exercises." Over time, this evolved into a distinct discipline initially performed on grass, hard surfaces, or thin felt mats.

Nowadays, floor gymnastics exercises are mostly learned on gym mats, floor tumbling tracks, or spring floors, often with the help of equipment like springboards, trampolines, airtracks, and more.

Floor gymnastics today is a sub-discipline of apparatus gymnastics and artistic gymnastics, but it is also a part of many other sports, such as sports acrobatics and various dance sports. It includes all individual techniques performed on the floor without the aid of trampolines or similar equipment. In addition movements like spins and jumps, which are minimally covered in this book, it involves rolling and flipping movements (roll, dive roll, somersault, cartwheel), balance exercises (headstand, handstand), and stretching exercises (bridge, splits, walkover).

Why Performing Floor Gymnastics?

If I ask myself whether I'd rather have dirty marks on the walls because my child constantly practices handstands against the bedroom wall, or if I'd prefer to take them to the eye doctor because they're glued to their phone screen 24/7, I'd choose the dirty walls.

Our society is increasingly shifting towards a sitting culture. It's no surprise. Even in school, the focus is primarily on intellectual development. I've never heard of a child repeating class due to sports, art, or music. These subjects are often given away as grades in primary school - apparently, they hold no real value.

Aside from being a massive waste of potential talent, this is very disappointing for children and teenagers who shine in these areas. I remember many students who struggled with subjects like writing or calculating. They were frustrated with the school routine, but excelled in sports and gained recognition from their peers. These children drew so much strength from their involvement in gymnastics that they managed to cope better with other subjects over time.

Floor gymnastics is a time-intensive activity that requires immense patience and almost endless endurance – qualities that children naturally possess if we don't discourage them by letting them rot in front of the TV or carting them around in strollers. Many children gain tremendous self-confidence from mastering various techniques. I vividly remember the thrill of balancing my first handstand—and I was already an adult at that time.

Besides providing self-confidence, gymnastics strengthens the entire body and demands a high level of spatial awareness, which is incredibly beneficial in scientific subjects.

Floor gymnastics can also foster social interaction. From experience, children love to compete with each other, whether it's seeing who can hold a handstand the longest, perform the best cartwheel, or achieve a deeper split. Moreover, it's a wonderful way to engage in self-directed activity away from media consumption.

In short, there are countless reasons to start with floor gymnastics, and much can be done without investing in expensive equipment, unlike some other hobbies. So, why not give it a try?

Principles for Learning Techniques

A word of caution: Floor gymnastics techniques come with inherent risks! While basic techniques might not be more dangerous than riding a bike, once you start performing airborne skills, there is always a risk of serious and lasting injury.

I strongly recommend the following:

- Learn techniques in order. It makes no sense to master the somersault before the roll or the back handspring before the handstand.
- Better to be over-prepared than under-prepared. Always have a partner who can safely spot you for difficult techniques, so they can catch you if necessary.
- Trust your instincts! From experience, I can say you won't master a technique if you don't believe you can. Even the best coach can't teach you a somersault if you're too stiff with fear.
- Only practice when you're feeling fit and know your limits. Injuries often arise not from inability but from carelessness. If you feel exhausted after ten somersaults, save the eleventh for another day.
- Have fun and be open to failure. Frustration is a poor companion and can lead to injury if you push too hard.
- Be aware of the risk of injury. Even with the best preparation and safety measures, you can still get seriously hurt while practicing gymnastics.

Helping and Spotting

I learned most of the techniques I know today without any assistance. This was simply because, as a very tall adult who started gymnastics, none of my coaches could safely spot me. This meant many painful landings on my back for me.

I wouldn't recommend this! Especially for children and teenagers, it's crucial to always have parents or strong adults help when attempting difficult techniques. The appropriate spotting techniques are detailed at the end of each section.

If a helper isn't available and club membership isn't an option, visiting a trampoline park with a „foam pit" is the best choice. These foam-filled pits are the only truly safe option for injury-free practice. Otherwise, a basic gym mat at home is a must have. A soft landing mat is even better to absorb harder falls. For jumping techniques, investing in a small airtrack (20 cm height) is recommended to provide additional height and easier learning.

The process of supporting involves three stages:

Assisting: The supporter helps from the start, reducing the effort needed and leads the gymnast trough the exercise.

Spotting: The supporter doesn't actively hold on unless necessary. His hands remain close to body parts that may lose balance or at critical points that need support.

Fall Protection: The supporter is within reach of the performer. His arms are actively extended and ready to catch. He gets active only to catch a foreseeable or immediate fall.

My advice is to provide as much support as necessary and as little as possible. Start with maximum assistance. As the gymnasts skills improve, the helper can gradually withdraw. If a technique is always performed with heavy support, there's a risk of becoming too reliant and not progressing to practicing alone.

The helper should always position himself close enough to intervene promptly. He should be familiar with the exercise and aware of the likely direction of a fall, without obstructing the performer. For complex elements that are harder to spot, it's crucial to practice spotting during preliminary exercises, if possible. This helps in developing a feel for the proper grip in a safe environment.

Conditional Preparation

Strength training is not a necessity in floor gymnastics but can be a valuable addition. For some techniques that are quite strength-intensive, I even recommend it. Otherwise, if you are physically fit, most exercises can be performed effectively through preparatory exercises and prior techniques. Consequently, I only introduce a few strength exercises here that can be done as a warm-up or in between sessions.

I strongly recommend regular stretching exercises. For many techniques, flexibility is not crucial, but for some, it is beneficial, and for others, it is absolutely necessary. For example, a back handspring requires excellent back and shoulder flexibility and ideally, the splits. Even for basic techniques like the handstand, you will achieve significantly better results if your shoulders have adequate mobility.

Strength

Floor gymnastics requires a lot of strength. I generally recommend a focused strength session after stretching or a more extensive one after technique training.

In floor gymnastics, you'll spend less time on preparation since each technique includes preparatory exercises that can also build the necessary strength. Therefore, it's possible to learn the strength aspects of floor gymnastics directly through the exercises themselves.

Common approaches to strength training include:

- Performing several sets of the same exercise consecutively, e.g., three sets of ten push-ups. Take a fixed break between sets.
- Pyramids. Use a fixed time interval, e.g., five minutes. Start with one repetition, then rest for the same duration as the repetition, then do two repetitions with a corresponding rest period, and so on. When you can no longer perform additional repetitions in sequence, start reducing the repetitions.
- A fixed short time interval, e.g., 30 seconds, in which you perform as many repetitions of an exercise as possible at maximum speed.

I've aimed to limit the selection of exercises to essential „must-haves" that should be manageable for any healthy person. Of course, it's also beneficial to seek additional reading or guidance and to build strength with a more comprehensive program.

Leg raises

This exercise strengthens the abdominal muscles.

Lie flat on your back. Try to press your lower back into the ground to minimize the arch. Lift your legs straight up and then slowly lower them back down.

You should aim to complete at least 10 repetitions of this exercise in a row, ideally 30.

Easier Variations:

To make the exercise easier, you can lift one leg at a time or keep your legs bent and extend them only after lifting.

Harder Variations:

Instead of letting your legs rest completely on the ground, keep them a few centimeters above the floor as you lower them, then lift them back up.
For an extra challenge, lift your pelvis at the top of the movement as well.

The Bird

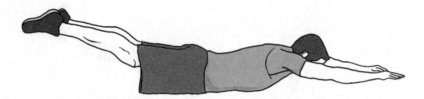

This is a static exercise to strengthen the back muscles, but it can also be performed dynamically.

Lie flat on your stomach, engage your back and glute muscles, and lift your legs, arms, and upper body off the ground. Try to raise your upper body as high as possible. Hold this position for as long as you can. Alternatively, you can hold the position for a few seconds, lower down, and then lift back up.

You should aim to hold this exercise for at least 30 seconds, ideally over a minute.

Easier Variation:

Extend your arms backward instead of forward, or lift only your upper body or only your legs.

Harder Variation:

Spread your arms and legs and then bring them back together, meanwhile holding the position statically.

The Boat

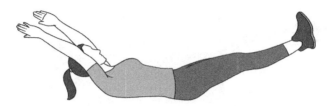

The reverse form of the flyer, which primarily trains the abdominal muscles. It's an excellent preparation for the handstand and numerous other techniques that require a strong core. This technique can be practiced statically or dynamically.

Lie flat on your back, press your lower back into the ground, and stretch out. Simultaneously lift your arms, legs, and upper body off the floor. Ideally, only your buttocks should still be touching the ground. Hold this position as long as you can, or perform the exercise dynamically by holding for a few seconds, lowering down, and then returning to the boat position.

You should aim to hold this exercise for at least 30 seconds, ideally over a minute.

Easier Variations:

Extend your arms forward instead of backward.
Slightly bend your legs.

Harder Variation:

Similar to the flyer, you can flap your arms and legs open and closed or move your legs up and down alternately without touching the ground.

The Bounce Jump

This exercise is part of my standard warm-up routine. It works all the muscles of the body and particularly enhances jumping power, making it essential for all jumping techniques.

Stand with your legs together, engage your core, and raise your arms as high as you can without arching your back. Jump from the balls of your feet, land without letting your heels touch the ground, and immediately perform the next jump by springing from your ankles.

There's no specific number of repetitions required for this exercise. Just focus on consistently improving your jump height.

The Frog Stand

The frog stand is excellent for training the shoulders and arms and is a great preparation for the handstand and headstand.

Squat down, spread your legs, and place your hands shoulder-width apart. Either press your knees against your elbows/upper arms or lean them directly against your upper arms. Try to shift your upper body forward, which will automatically lift your feet off the ground, and balance your weight on your hands.

If you can't hold this position at all, try to accumulate seconds by holding it briefly but repeatedly.
You should aim to hold this exercise for at least 10 seconds, ideally 30 seconds.

Easier Variation:
Keep one foot on the ground or balance on your toes with that foot to reduce the weight as needed.

Harder Variation:
Instead of resting your legs on your arms, place them between your arms and attempt the same position. This variation requires significantly more strength.

The squat

A classic strengthening exercise that targets both the thighs and glutes.

Stand with your feet shoulder-width apart, turn your toes out slightly, and push your hips back and down. Make sure your knees move as little as possible forward. To balance, you can lean your straight upper body slightly forward. The static variation, where you hold the lowest position for as long as possible, is also highly beneficial.

You should aim to complete at least 30 repetitions, ideally 50.

Easier Variation:

If this exercise is challenging, use a chair or similar for support, or don't squat to deep.

Harder Variation:

Perform the exercise on one leg, extending the other leg forward without touching the ground.

The plank

Another timeless classic that engages the entire body and is highly recommended.

Lie on your stomach. Place your toes on the ground and rest on your forearms. Lift yourself into the plank position. Be sure to keep your core engaged and avoid arching your back.

You should aim to hold this exercise for at least one minute, ideally three minutes or more.

Easier Variation:

You can support your arms on an elevated surface to reduce the pressure on your shoulders.

Harder Variations:

- Move your forearms further ahead.
- Lift one leg at a time, keeping it straight.
- Place your legs on an elevated surface.
- Transition from a plank position to a push-up position and back.

Flexibility

Some people are naturally more flexible than others. As a coach, I've met children who were as flexible as cooked spaghetti and others whose range of motion was less than my own.

For floor gymnastics, a certain level of flexibility is required to perform some techniques correctly. For example, you can't achieve a completely straight handstand if you can't extend your arms straight up to your ears. A back handspring is much harder to learn without a certain degree of back flexibility, and executing a free cartwheel without having at least some split flexibility is nearly impossible.

That's why I've put together a routine to stretch the key muscle groups. For clarity, I won't go into detail about each exercise; the images should be self-explanatory.

Ideally, hold each position for at least ten seconds, better twenty to thirty seconds. To deepen the stretch, breathe deeply and push further into the stretch as you exhale.

Unilateral stretches (e.g., stretching towards one leg) should of course be performed on both sides.

Basic techniques

These techniques are usually learnable on your own. Assistance can be useful for achieving faster progress but is not strictly necessary.

To avoid hard landings, it's advisable to use at least a gym mat during practice. When purchasing a mat, make sure it is not too soft.

For exercises like the handstand, it can be very problematic if your hands sink into the mat while practicing. Sinking can overstretch the wrists and make balancing nearly impossible.

Soft mats are therefore recommended only for cushioning falls (e.g., placing them in the direction of the back of the practitioner). If practicing on an Airtrack, it should be inflated as firmly as possible.

Basic techniques

The Forward Roll

Description

The forward roll is typically the first exercise that most children encounter, often starting with the somersault. For young children, it can often seem like an insurmountable challenge because their head is still proportionally large compared to their body. By the age of six, most children can overcome this issue with proper technique. However, even then, the roll can be more difficult for them compared to adults, whose arms extend much further over their heads.

Preliminary Exercises

To roll at all, usually, no extensive preparatory exercises are necessary. However, a good forward roll requires significant strength and technique; otherwise, a hard fall onto the neck or lower back is likely. I recommend practicing the roll to perfection, as it becomes incredibly important later on for techniques like the headstand, handstand, or when failing a cartwheel. Mastering the roll helps you roll out safely rather than crashing to the ground.

The back swing

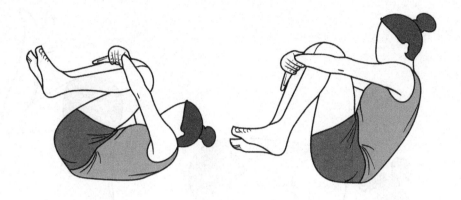

This exercise focuses on learning to maintain a rounded back. Lie on your back, pull your legs towards your chest, and rock back and forth. Ideally, you should aim to come to your feet from this rocking motion without using your hands. If you lack the necessary strength to hold your legs close to your body, you can initially use your hands to assist in holding them in place.

The tuck handstand

This exercise strengthens the arms and helps maintain the correct rolling position. Start in a squat position and place your hands slightly in front of your feet. Then, jump off both feet, keeping your thighs pressed against your torso, and try to hold this position for a few seconds. It might be challenging to hold this position initially. Alternatively, practice the exercise repeatedly with brief holds at the highest position.

Rolling from an Elevated Surface

This exercise helps you learn how to properly support yourself during a roll and is an excellent preparatory step for rolling out of a handstand from a certain height. Find a platform about hip height (such as the edge of a bed). Lie face down on the platform and slide your upper body over the edge. As soon as possible, place your hands on the ground, tuck your chin to your chest, and roll down slowly and controlled, bending your arms and placing the back of your neck on the floor.

Once you start the roll, pull your bent legs towards your chest to maintain a rounded position.

Rolling from a Slope

This exercise is usually unnecessary if you have diligently completed the previous exercises. Additionally, it can be challenging to set up at home. You can use an inclined surface like a wedge (e.g., a slanted cushion, a springboard) placed under a gymnastics mat or blanket. Make sure the slope is not too steep.

Stand at the highest point of the inclined surface or just in front of it. Place your hands in front of you, tuck your chin to your chest, and roll down the slope, placing your neck between your hands. Try to use the momentum from the slope to stand up without using your hands.

Rolling onto an Elevated Surface

This exercise increases the difficulty of the roll and is particularly useful if gymnasts can roll but do not properly support themselves with their arms. This often results in uncontrolled rolls. To assess this, you can have the gymnast perform a roll on a hard surface; if it hurts, they lack control, and this exercise can help enforce proper rolling technique.

Stand in front of an elevation (approximately knee-height). Place your hands far from the edge to prevent falling off, push off strongly with your feet, tuck your chin to your chest, and pull your thighs towards your torso. Place your neck on the elevation and roll over it until you stand up on your feet.

As an alternative, you can initially adjust the elevation so that your feet land back on the ground after one roll.

Execution of the forward roll

Go into a squat and place your hands shoulder-width apart slightly in front of you on the ground. Press actively against the floor with your fingers pointing forward.

Shift your weight onto your hands by extending your legs.

Tuck your chin to your chest, push off from your feet, and place your neck/upper back on the ground. Try to maintain a rounded position until you are back on your feet. Keep your thighs close to your torso throughout the roll.

After the roll, stand up without using your hands for support.

Tips

- A fast roll is not always a good roll. Speed often just compensates poor technique.
- Perform the roll as slowly and controlled as possible. If you can stand up on your feet without using your hands for support, you have mastered it.
- To check if your roll is truly stable, try it on a hard wooden floor. If you experience pain, you may need more arm strength or better rounding in your roll. (Note: Small children might not yet be able to achieve perfect rounding due to their body proportions.)

Spotting

A roll typically doesn't require spotting. However, you can assist the gymnast by placing a hand on his shoulder, which helps reduce the effort needed to transition into the roll and allows for more controlled arm movement. This also helps prevent the gymnast from landing hard on his neck if the roll is executed incorrectly.

The Headstand

Description

The headstand introduces the first balance exercise that forms the basis for the handstand and also builds strength for the cartwheel.

To perform the headstand, position your hands and head in a triangular formation on the floor and align your body vertically above your head.

The three contact points make balancing the headstand significantly easier. However, the entry into the headstand can be technically challenging, as ideally, it should not be performed with momentum.

Preliminary Exercises

The headstand is generally a „try and error" technique. The risk of injury is relatively low, especially if you use a mat, as the fall height is minimal. However, there are a few ways to make this technique easier and to get a feel for it.

To achieve the necessary strength, exercises for the core muscles are recommended. In rare cases, training the neck muscles might be appropriate, but from my experience, this is necessary only about 1% of the time. On the contrary, I've seen many children attempt the headstand without using their hands for fun—though this is not necessarily advisable.

Headstand with Knees Resting

Go into a squat position. Place your hands shoulder-width apart in front of you and position your head in front of them. Your hands and head should form a triangle. Rest your left knee on your bent left arm. Once you can hold this position, place your right knee on your right arm.

Once you can hold this position steadily for a while, try to lift both knees slightly off your arms and stabilize this position.

Climbing into the headstand

Kneel in front of a wall. Place your hands shoulder-width apart approximately beside your knees. Rest the top of your head on the ground in front of your hands, forming a triangle with your head and hands. You should be able to see your hands.

Press your hands firmly into the ground and climb the wall with your feet. At the highest point, push one leg vertically and continue to support yourself with the other leg. When you feel secure, try to move the second leg into the vertical position as well. Keep your core engaged to avoid arching your lower back.

Headstand from an Elevated Surface

For many, the most challenging part of the headstand is lifting the feet off the ground with control. Many people end up rolling or swing up because they haven't mastered the correct technique yet. A wall behind you, by the way, usually doesn't help and often exacerbates the problem!

Find an elevated surface (e.g., your bed) that is no higher than the length of your torso. Lie down on it and slide over the edge. Place your hands and head on the ground in the usual triangle formation and arch your back by moving your legs further towards the edge. As you feel your weight pulling you backward, lift your bent legs and bring your thighs close to vertical. You need to stop before you feel like you're going to topple over, and fix this position by engaging your core muscles and pressing your hands firmly into the ground.

Headstand against a wall

Once you are comfortable with the above techniques, you can use a wall for support. An even better option is a soft elevation that supports your upper back but doesn't allow you to lean your feet against it.

Start by squatting in front of a wall. Place your hands a little distance from the wall and position your head slightly away from the wall.

Walk your feet towards your torso so that your back curves and makes contact with the wall. Once you feel your weight pulling your feet upward, use the pressure from your hands and engage your back muscles to lift your bent legs. You may need to step away from the wall a bit first.

As your feet touch the wall, try to straighten them and push them upward, aiming to get your legs to a position where they no longer make contact with the wall.

Execution of the headstand

Begin by squatting down and placing your hands shoulder-width apart on the ground. Position your head with the top of your skull facing down about a hand's length in front of your hands, forming a triangle with them.

Walk your feet as close as possible to your hands, causing your back to bend. Once your body weight shifts enough towards your back and you feel that your legs are „weightless," lift them bent and without momentum until your thighs are vertical.

Straighten your back and extend your legs. Make sure not to lift them completely vertical but rather allow them to hang slightly towards your belly. Adjust the imbalance by pressing down with your hands and engaging your core muscles.

Once you have mastered this position, you can try coming in position with your legs straight and spread apart, and later, bringing them together while lifting them upward. These variations are more challenging and require you to bend your back more initially.

Tips
- You should never attempt a headstand with momentum. Doing so significantly increases the risk of falling into an arch and tipping over. Unlike a handstand, you cannot create counterpressure with your hands in a headstand.
- Keep your hands in place. Many people try to prevent tipping over by positioning their hands beside their head, but this often leads to falling forward instead.
- For some, it may be easier initially to vary the ascent by keeping one leg on the ground while raising the other leg straight into the final position, then bringing the other leg up afterward.

Spotting

There are two effective ways to assist a headstand:

The first method involves standing behind the gymnast, holding his hips to support the ascent and prevent tipping over. Additionally, you can use your shins to support the upper back. It's important to initially stand at a distance to allow the necessary bending of the back.

As the gymnast becomes more proficient, it makes more sense to position yourself to the side and only secure the final position or assist the ascent on one leg if needed. Once the legs are extended, the helper should grasp one leg with both hands to help with balancing. Gradually, the helper can reduce contact and only intervene to prevent tipping over.

Basic techniques

The Handstand

Description

The handstand is arguably the quintessential exercise in gymnastics. Mastering it to the point of true stability often takes years of practice, and it offers so many variations that an entire book could be dedicated to it alone. The ability to balance your weight on your hands is not only crucial as a standalone skill but also serves as a foundation for many other techniques. Therefore, it is highly recommended to prioritize the handstand over other advanced techniques.

Preliminary Exercises

The handstand is a technically demanding skill. Initially, it's most important to develop the strength needed to hold the position for a sufficient amount of time. Once you have that, you can focus on fine-tuning your balance on your hands and practicing the classic kick-up into the handstand.

For some children, there's no fear of falling onto their back. I've seen many practice handstands on grass until they learned to roll or turn out of the fall on their own, thereby avoiding frequent falls. Generally, I wouldn't discourage such daring children, but it's ideal to provide them with a soft mat. Nonetheless, even these children should invest time in preliminary exercises to work on their proper form.

Handstand with an Elevation

This exercise is particularly useful for developing strength and the correct form for the handstand. For very anxious or less athletic individuals, it's recommended to start with a slight elevation (like a bed or couch) and only use a wall when you feel more secure.

Position yourself with your back to a wall or elevation. Ensure the surrounding area, especially in the direction you will fall, is clear for about two meters. Ideally, place a mat in the direction of the fall.

Climb up the wall or elevation with your feet and move your hands closer to it. At first, it's advisable to keep a little distance between your hands and the wall to reduce the risk of falling.

Once you're in the handstand position, straighten your entire body, press out from your shoulders, engage your core, and avoid arching your lower back. If your hands are not directly against the wall, try to slightly bend your hips so your torso is completely vertical and only your legs lean against the wall. If you're using just an elevation, place your feet or lower legs on it and also aim to get your torso as vertical as possible.

One-Legged Wall Handstand

Once you have mastered the previous exercise, it's time to focus on straightening your handstand and getting a feel for the correct position. Additionally, this exercise will help you start balancing with your hands.

Begin by climbing into a handstand against the wall and move your hands as close to the wall as possible without risking falling over. (A hand's length away from the wall is sufficient.)

Now, perform what you might have already done in the previous exercise with both legs. Lift one leg off the wall and extend it straight up. Use the other leg to push yourself forward until your torso and arms form a straight line.

Actively press with your fingers into the ground to prevent tipping over. Once you feel confident, briefly lift your other leg off the wall and immediately press back with your fingers. The goal of this exercise is not necessarily to hold a free handstand but to be able to push yourself back toward your stomach.

If you want to work on holding the handstand, try keeping your foot away from the wall for a longer period without tipping over. Using a mat is advisable to cushion any potential falls.

At this early stage, it's not recommended to align both legs vertically, as you might arch your lower back and fall over.

Handstand Roll-Out

It is generally recommended to practice rolling out of a handstand before attempting a free handstand. Alternatively, you could start with learning the cartwheel and then progress to the more complex technique to turn off from the handstand with a cartwheel.

Climb into a handstand against the wall, keeping at least a hand's length distance from it. Bend your hips so that your torso and arms are in a vertical line. Slowly and carefully bend your arms and tuck your chin to your chest. Place the back of your neck on the floor, arch your back, and, if necessary, push lightly off the wall to roll forward onto the ground.

A yoga mat is essential for this exercise, as rolling over the spine can be uncomfortable initially.

It is crucial to perform this exercise slowly and controlled. The faster you roll, the greater the risk of landing on your lower back.

Tuck-Handstand

The tuck handstand is an excellent exercise for preparing the free handstand, as it allows you to practice balancing and rolling out from a lower height. In general, the tuck handstand can be harder to stabilize, so it's not necessary to master it completely before learning the handstand. However, once you can do the tuck handstand, the handstand itself becomes less challenging.

Start by squatting down and placing your hands on the floor at about knee height. Jump off both feet without straightening your legs. In your initial attempts, you may not land in the correct position right away. Gradually increase your jump power, focus on pushing back with your fingers if you swing too much, and try to align your torso and arms into a straight line while keeping your legs bent.

If you have a mat, you can also practice rolling out from this position.

Execution of the Handstand

Stand in a lunge position. Place your hands shoulder-width apart on the ground about a step in front of you. Use your front leg to push off the ground with force, and swing your back leg straight up. Once you are vertical, bring the lower leg up.

Engage your core to prevent overbalancing, and balance yourself solely through pressure and adjustment in your fingers.

Alternatively, but more difficult, you can enter the handstand by first jumping into a tuck handstand with both legs and then straightening them.

For some, it's also easier to place the hands in the lunge position, lift the swinging leg straight up, and then achieve the handstand with a weak push-off from the standing leg. This technique is generally more challenging as it requires more strength, but it helps prevent overbalancing.

Tips

The transition from preliminary exercises to the free handstand is usually challenging because people often lack a sense of how strongly to push off. Additionally, there is fear of falling painfully when attempting this technique. Therefore, I recommend initially practicing the handstand by kicking up against a wall. You should place your hands directly in front of the wall and try to avoid touching it, as touching it means you are not in the optimal hand-stand position. This exercise helps you practice applying just the right amount of kicking energy.

Secondly, the scissor handstand has proven effective. In this technique, you first swing only the kicking leg while keeping the standing leg bent or extended downward. This will likely cause you to fall back towards your stomach repeatedly at first, allowing you to gradually get accustomed to the end position.

The more challenging method is to first swing the kicking leg high, then bring the standing leg up, but simultaneously pull the kicking leg back down. This creates a scissor-like movement and keeps you in the fully extended, straight handstand position for a shorter period, significantly reducing the risk of falling.

Spotting

The spotter should ideally never stand behind the performer to avoid the risk of injury to both individuals.

As a spotter, stand to the side of the performer, specifically on the side of the kicking leg, as this leg goes up first. Catch the kicking leg at its highest position with both hands and prevent the performer from overbalancing.
If you feel the performer is starting to collapse, support them by pulling upward and either assist them into a roll by guiding the movement or push them towards their stomach to help them come down safely.

The Cartwheel

Description

The cartwheel is one of the most common exercises, often learned by many at a very young age through trial and error. It is a prerequisite for the roundoff and is therefore essential for learning advanced combinations such as roundoff-Flick or roundoff-somersault.

Essentially, it is just a fleeting handstand that is swung sideways and then swung back in the direction of movement.

While the cartwheel can be learned using the trial and error method, working through the appropriate preliminary exercises can help avoid some unpleasant falls on the back.

Preliminary Exercises

For adults, it's advisable to start by learning the handstand, as they may sometimes lack the strength to hold their weight on their hands. Additionally, a fall can be much more uncomfortable compared to younger children.

The Squat Turn

This exercise focuses on building the necessary strength to briefly support yourself on your hands and getting a feel for the direction of movement.

It's recommended to perform this over a small elevation or at least a marking on the floor.

Start by going into a squat position and place your hands diagonally (to the left or right) in front of you. Jump in the squat position in the direction you've chosen, keeping your hands on the ground (or on your elevation), and then repeat the movement in the opposite direction.

The goal is to get your hips as high as possible - ideally, directly above your hands.

One-Legged Squat Turn

Once you can perform the squat turn with sufficient height, it's time to learn the correct leg movement. For this, you'll make a small adjustment:

If you place your hands to the left, extend your right leg forward and your left leg backward. Jump off the right leg and swing the left leg up. You should land first on the left leg and then on the right.

If you place your hands to the right, do the opposite.

The Squat Wheel

Position yourself as you would for the one-legged squat turn, but this time, slightly extend the rear leg during the jump. The front leg should be placed straight forward, and as well place your hands in a line, just like in a proper cartwheel. Start this exercise from a squat position, then try it from standing. Place your hands one after the other to get a feel for the correct cartwheel.

Push off only with the front leg (supporting leg), and swing the rear leg (swinging leg) vigorously upward. Land first on the swinging leg, then on the supporting leg. Your swinging leg should now be in front, and the supporting leg behind.

You might notice that you do it better on one side. You can either practice both sides or focus on turning your hands to the right (right leg forward) or to the left (left leg forward). Remember: if the left leg is forward, place the left hand down first; if the right leg is forward, do the opposite.

Once you master this exercise, try to extend and spread both legs while swinging so that your legs land one after the other, rather than simultaneously.

Execution of the cartwheel

Take a large step forward and place the same-side hand (right leg forward - right hand, left leg forward - left hand) on the ground. Rotate the hand outward so that the fingers point to the side. Push off from the front leg and swing the other leg vigorously upward while keeping it straight. Place your second hand slightly away from your first hand on the ground, spread your legs as wide as possible in the air, and rotate your torso in the direction of movement.

Allow your feet to fall one after the other (swinging leg first, then supporting leg) towards your stomach, and land in a lunge position. At the same time, raise your arms from below to above, keeping them tense. This step should not be underestimated, as improper arm positioning can be difficult to correct later and can hinder learning the roundoff.

Tips

- Practice the wheel as long as necessary in a tucked position. This increases the difficulty but also reduces the fear of falling.
- Engage your core during the exercise to prevent arching your back. This is the most common reason for falling on your back while doing the wheel.
- Sometimes, it is helpful to perform the wheel from an elevation initially to have more time to swing your legs.
- Practice the wheel on a line or in front of a wall to perfect the straight execution.

Spotting

As a spotter, position yourself next to the gymnast exactly where he place his hands. If he moves his right foot forward, stand on his right side; if he moves his left foot forward, stand on his left side. Grip your partner's hips and guide him through the movement, preventing him from tipping onto his back.

Spotting is rarely necessary for the cartwheel, but it can help by applying pressure to the lower back to prevent the gymnast from falling onto his back.

The Bridge

Description

The bridge exercise involves lifting the hips from a lying position until the arms are nearly vertical and the legs are straight.

For some gymnasts, this exercise is not very challenging due to their remarkable flexibility. For others, it requires intense training, and some may not be able to learn the bridge at all due to a lack of shoulder flexibility.

The bridge is a valuable component if you plan to learn the back handspring and the back walkover. For the walkover, it is even essential.

Preliminary Exercises

Firstly, for the bridge exercise, all stretching exercises that increase your shoulder mobility, stretch your back, and also your thigh muscles are beneficial. Generally, I recommend pre-stretching these muscles before performing the bridge to achieve better results.

There are only a few truly effective preliminary exercises for the bridge, which I will outline below.

Shoulder Bridge

Lie on your back and draw your feet towards your buttocks. Place your arms by your sides. Press your feet firmly into the ground and lift your hips up towards your torso. You can then interlace your hands under your back and try to squeeze your shoulder blades together. Hold this position for at least 30 seconds.

This exercise should be achievable for everyone, even if you can't yet perform the full bridge. You will need to do it daily over an extended period to improve your flexibility and make progress.

It is also suitable as a warm-up exercise for the bridge.

Wrestler's Bridge

This classic preliminary exercise is particularly helpful if you still lack the necessary shoulder flexibility and/or strength to hold the bridge position.

Lie on your back, drawing your feet close to your buttocks, and place your hands palm-down beside your ears. Lift your hips up towards your torso and press yourself up using your arms. Slightly arch your head back, using the top of your head to stabilize yourself in this position.

Be sure not to remove the pressure from your hands and rely solely on your head for support.

You can also try pushing yourself a bit higher so that your head briefly loses contact with the ground, making the exercise more dynamic.

This exercise is useful for actively working on shoulder flexibility and the strength needed to press into the bridge. Like the shoulder bridge, you will need to perform this exercise regularly over an extended period to achieve the desired results.

Bridge with Elevation

Place your feet on a stable elevation (e.g., a couch, low table, or mattress). Lie your back flat on the ground. Position your hands beside your ears and push your hips up. At the same time, press your arms further upwards. This position is helpful if your shoulder flexibility is not yet sufficient but will require increased shoulder strength, making it also a good strength-training exercise for your shoulders.

You can also perform this exercise dynamically by slowly lowering your shoulders back down and then pushing yourself back up.

Execution of the bridge

Lie on your back and pull your feet as close to your buttocks as possible. Place your hands beside your ears. Push your hips up towards your torso, and simultaneously fully extend your arms. By stretching your legs, you can further press into the shoulder stretch.

Tips

- Practicing the bridge on your toes can make the exercise easier, but it's more effective to use a stable elevation for support.
- To check if you have the necessary flexibility, stand with your back against a wall. Press your lower back against the wall, engage your abdominal muscles, and try to place your hands overhead against the wall with your arms fully extended.

Spotting

Spotting can be useful for the bridge in two ways. Firstly, it helps the performer go deeper into the stretch, and secondly, it reduces the effort required by providing upward pressure.

As a spotter, position yourself at the head of the performer with your feet placed slightly beside their head. The performer will place their hands on your feet. Grab under their shoulders and assist them in pushing up.

In the final position, you can support the stretch by gently pulling the performer towards your legs.

Advanced Techniques

In my experience, these techniques can also be learned independently with the appropriate effort. Only the round-off and the dive roll pose a certain risk of injury, which can be drastically minimized through preliminary exercises.

All of these exercises require extended practice time, and I strongly recommend mastering all the basic techniques (excluding the bridge) before attempting the advanced exercises.

A soft mat is mandatory, especially for the dive roll!

The Roundoff

Description

The round-off is a challenging follow-up element to the cartwheel and serves to accelerate into techniques like the back handspring or backflip.

In this technique, you perform a cartwheel with closed legs and over-rotated hands, landing powerfully on both feet in the opposite direction of the movement.

You don't necessarily need to master this exercise before the others in this chapter; rather, you should practice it intermittently. It typically takes a considerable amount of time to master this technique to the point where it can be effectively combined with other techniques.

Preliminary Exercises

Training this exercise to perfection can be a very lengthy process. Once you have mastered the basic form, you can refine the finer points through constant repetition.

Cartwheel with Both Feet Landing

Perform a cartwheel as slowly as possible. Initially, try to land your feet one after the other directly next to each other. Once that works, make both feet touch the ground simultaneously.

When you can do this well, start turning your hands further. This means placing your hands not side by side at a 90° angle to your body, but rather positioning the first hand in the opposite direction of the movement and placing the second hand next to it. At first, this will be challenging, but the faster you swing into the roundoff, the easier it will be to place your hands correctly.

To gain additional speed, you can add a small hop before the roundoff. Jump with both feet and swing your arms forward. Land in a lunge position and use the momentum from the jump to gain more swing for the roundoff.

Cartwheel into Handstand

For this exercise, you should be comfortable with the free handstand. Perform a regular cartwheel and interrupt it at the highest point so that your lead leg meets the push off leg at the top, and you end up in a handstand. Ideally, let your legs fall simultaneously toward your stomach.

Once you can do this, try it while turning your hands further out, as you should for the roundoff. If you have a large, soft mat (or a mattress) available, you can also practice this against a wall, allowing your feet to touch the wall (or the soft surface) at the end.

Handstand Snap Down

To practice the handstand snap down, begin by kicking up into a handstand against a wall. Ensure your hands are positioned far enough from the wall so that your back is slightly arched. If a wall is not available, you can perform this exercise freely, but it's ideal to have a spotter to prevent you from falling over. Once in position, forcefully bring your legs down to the floor while keeping them straight. This movement, known as a „snap down," must be executed with maximum speed. As you master the snap down, add a push from your shoulders as you bring your legs down, causing both your hands and feet to momentarily lift off the ground. Using a raised surface can be helpful for this exercise, as it gives you more time to execute the powerful snap down. Practice the snap down repeatedly to build the necessary speed and strength in your shoulders and core.

Execution of the roundoff

From a lunge position, place your right or left hand on the ground, rotated more than 90 degrees, similar to how you would for a cartwheel. Swing your lead leg up while your push off leg drives you upward. Place your second hand next to the first, bringing your push off leg to meet your lead leg, forming a brief handstand with a slightly arched back. Push off with your shoulders and simultaneously snap your legs down powerfully. Ideally, your heels should not touch the ground as you use the momentum for a high jump. This energy will then be used to perform a back handspring or a back tuck.

Tips

- The round-off becomes easier with more momentum. Optimize your takeoff or combine it with a run-up of 2-3 steps.
- To perform a back handspring afterward, place your feet as close to your hands as possible. For a back tuck, position them further away.
- Core tension is crucial for this move. If you arch your back too much, your leg snap will lack power.

Spotting

As a spotter, you should focus on supporting the preliminary exercises by positioning yourself beside the gymnast and assisting them in maintaining their handstand.

For the roundoff itself, constant spotting isn't necessary. However, when practicing the roundoff with a stretch jump, it's useful to place a hand on the gymnast's back at the end to prevent them from being thrown off by their own momentum.

Make sure to position yourself at the back of the gymnast to avoid getting hit by his legs if the roundoff isn't perfectly aligned.

The One-Arm Wheel

Description

The one-arm wheel is a more advanced version of the regular wheel. Instead of using both hands, you place only one hand on the ground. This can be done with either the near or far hand, though the far hand is generally more challenging for most gymnasts. The far hand version serves as a preparatory exercise for the free wheel, making it particularly valuable for progress.

Preliminary Exercises

As a preparatory exercise, you should first focus on performing the standard wheel as quickly as possible, aiming to swing the lead leg with more force and bring it back down promptly. This reduces the effort required from your hands. It can also be beneficial to practice the wheel from a hop (as in the roundoff). Initially, try to place the second hand as late as possible and gradually move this timing further back until you can complete the wheel with just one hand. Practicing this exercise from an elevated surface can also be helpful.

Execution of the One-Arm Cartwheel

Start as you would with a standard wheel and try to push off as powerfully as possible from your push off leg, swinging the lead leg vigorously overhead. Place either the near hand (easier option) or the far hand (more challenging option) as you would in a normal wheel and perform the wheel as usual, but with only one hand.

Tips

- The better your split is, the easier it will be to bring the lead leg back down to the ground as quickly as possible.
- For some, it can be helpful to place the unused hand on the back. However, this can also increase the fear of falling.
- Start practicing the one-arm cartwheel from an elevated surface to minimize the time your hand is under load and to „fall" into the final position more safely.

Spotting

The spotting for the one-arm wheel is similar to the spotting for the regular wheel.

The Forearm Stand

Description

The forearm stand is technically similar to the handstand and head-stand. In this position, you balance on your forearms while keeping your feet in the air. Your back is usually arched. This position stabilizes more through the alignment of the upper body rather than through balancing on the forearms.

Typically, this exercise can be performed with a strongly arched back so that the feet nearly reach the head. Some practitioners also do it in a split. Both approaches not only enhance the aesthetic effect but also help with balancing the forearm stand.

Preliminary Exercises

The preliminary exercises for the forearm stand are similar to those for the handstand. The key is to learn the end position gradually without frequently falling to the ground.

Forearm Stand Climbing

Squat down with your back facing a wall. Place your forearms side by side on the floor. Climb the wall with your legs, extending one leg fully upwards while the other leg remains in contact with the wall for stability. You can try to lightly push off with the wall leg to get a feel for the final position. With practice – and ideally, a mat under your back – you can transition from this exercise into the full position.

Forearm Stand Against the Wall

Place your forearms side by side on the ground, keeping your hands close to the wall. Lift your feet and press your lower back upward with your feet. You can rest your lower back against the wall for extra support. Extend one leg upward and slightly bend it. Gently push off with the second leg and use the bent leg against the wall to stabilize yourself, preventing yourself from tipping over. Now, slightly arch your back so that only your feet are in contact with the wall. You can try to break contact with the wall from this position to practice the free forearm stand.

Execution of the Forearm Stand

Place your forearms shoulder-width apart on the floor. Alternatively, you can form a triangle with your forearms, though this will reduce your base of support. Place both feet on the ground and lift your hips as high as possible. Extend one leg upward and gently hop with the other leg to follow.

Usually, you'll need to slightly arch your back to maintain stability. Engage your core to avoid excessive arching and tipping over. Press firmly into the floor with your hands to prevent tipping.

If needed, you can practice the forearm stand in a split position, using the movement of your legs to find balance.

Tips

- The forearm stand is very challenging to stabilize solely with your arms. Practice gently moving your legs to correct any imbalance.
- In the forearm stand, keep your head in a neutral position; otherwise, it will touch the ground, which would resemble a yoga-style headstand.
- Just like with the headstand, the forearm stand should never be done with a jump. This greatly increases the risk of tipping over, which is much more unpleasant in the forearm stand compared to the headstand.

Spotting

Spotting for the forearm stand is similar to that for the handstand. It's crucial to prevent the turner from tipping backward, as rolling out of this position is nearly impossible.

The Jump Roll

Description

The jump roll, which is the best preliminary exercise for a forward somersault, differs from the regular roll due to its flight phase. By performing a two-legged jump, you reach a position similar to that of a handstand dismount. The jump roll can be executed with varying distances: it can be performed over a long distance or with more height, which is beneficial for learning the salto.

Preliminary Exercises

The main issue most people have with the jump roll is the fear of landing on their head. Because of this, many beginners struggle with gaining the necessary height. Therefore, the preliminary exercises focus on mastering the transition from the flight phase to the roll. Additionally, these exercises help develop the strength needed to control the roll after the flight phase. Often, the jump roll is practiced only on soft mats, which can cause turners to land hard on their back. Once the technique is well mastered, only standard mats should be used as the surface.

Roll on an Elevated Surface

Create an elevated surface for practice. Ideally, this would be a mound of soft mats, but if that's not available, a bed, couch, or something similar with a large, soft landing area can work as well. If you have no option for such an elevation, skip this preliminary exercise.

Stand in front of the elevated surface, place your hands side by side on it, and then jump and perform a normal roll onto it.
If this feels easy, try adding a hop (as seen in the roundoff) or a few steps of running before your jump. Ideally, you should aim to jump first and then place your hands on the elevated surface.

The gold standard - if you're elevated surface makes it possible – would be to execute the roll on the elevated surface but land with your feet on the ground.

Regardless of your level, make sure to tuck your chin to your chest as you place your hands down. Your arms should be firmly engaged, guiding you into the roll in a controlled manner rather than collapsing weakly.

Roll from an Elevated Surface

For this exercise, a bed or a couch works perfectly. The higher the elevation, the more effective the practice will be.

Lie flat on your elevated surface and move toward the edge so that you can place your hands on the floor.

Slide further to the edge, keeping your body engaged and your head tucked in. Roll off the edge as slowly as possible. It's wise to have a mat or something similar on the floor to prevent injury.

Rolling Over an Obstacle

This exercise is particularly helpful if you can perform the jump roll but struggle to get high enough.

Start by using an obstacle, such as a pile of pillows. You can keep it low initially.

First, reach over the obstacle and roll yourself off. Next, try to reach over with your hands but don't touch the floor, using a small hop to transition into the roll. Finally, attempt to grab over the obstacle only after you've jumped over it.

By increasing the height of the obstacle, you can practice achieving a higher jump in your roll.

Execution of the Jump Roll

From a running start with hop, only hop, or from a standing position, jump with both legs. Extend your arms forward towards your head, keeping your body tight, legs straight, and your hips slightly angled.

As soon as your hands touch the ground, press firmly against it to slow yourself down. Gradually sink into your arms and tuck your head to your chest. Bend your hips more than in a handstand roll, place your neck on the ground, and complete the roll.

Tips

- Keep your legs as straight as possible during the roll to avoid over-rotating and landing on your upper back.
- Try not to reach straight down but rather in the direction of your movement to give your roll more distance.
- If you're not jumping with enough power initially, bend your hips more to still complete the roll, or you might end up landing on your head.

Spotting

Securing the forward roll is significantly more challenging than a static exercise like the handstand. However, if you can lift the gymnast comfortably, it usually works well even with less experienced practitioners.

To get a feel for spotting, start by gripping the gymnast's hips with the hand closest to them and their lower back with the other hand before he begins the roll. Guide his movement and especially support them when they place their hands on the ground. This helps reduce the impact and allows you to slow him down if he collapses into his arms too quickly.

For a dynamic spot, I generally use the far hand. After the jump or just before, use this hand to press into the angle between his hips and abdomen. Since the gymnast's legs are bent, you can slow down his movement by applying pressure to his hips/thighs. Your arm also acts as a pivot point. If needed, your closer hand can hold the gymnast's thigh from behind to provide additional stability.

Alternatively, as shown in the illustration, you can grip both the thigh and shoulder to prevent sudden collapsing of the arms by controlling the shoulder.

The Backward Roll

Description

The backward roll mirrors the forward roll in its movement pattern but is a significantly more complex technique. After setting down backward, the feet are brought over the shoulders. With a strong push from the hands, the gymnast completes the roll and transitions into a squat position.

Preliminary Exercises

The movement sequence of this technique requires minimal preliminary practice. The key is having the necessary strength at the right time to transition from the back position into the squat. Therefore, it is essential to be able to perform a handstand or several clean push-ups before starting the practice.

Rolling Over a Slope

This exercise can be performed either over a sloped surface or from a slight elevation. For the sloped surface, sit at the highest point, place your hands by your ears with palms facing up, tuck your chin to your chest, and roll backward down the incline.

For the elevation, lie on your back with your shoulders at the edge of the elevated surface. Then sit up so that you can roll back and place your hands exactly where the edge of the elevation is.

This exercise helps reduce the effort needed for the push-off and allows you to practice the movement under easier conditions. Still, try to actively push off with your hands to transition into the squat. The elevation doesn't need to be very high; the smaller the elevation, the more effort you'll need to put in yourself.

Rolling Backward into a Push-Up Position

This exercise is generally more challenging than the backward roll itself, but it helps to develop the ability to quickly move your legs upward while applying pressure with your hands. Perform the roll as described under „Execution," but aim to move your legs swiftly backward and upward. At the same time, exert pressure with your hands so that you land in a push-up position with your legs extended.

Execution of the Backward Roll

Start from a standing or crouching position. Place your hands by your ears with your palms facing upward. Lower your torso, bend your back, and make yourself as compact as possible. Roll backward, placing your neck on the ground and tucking your head to your chest.

As soon as your feet pass over your head, push off the floor with both hands powerfully. Bring your legs into a crouch if they were previously extended or only slightly bent, and land in a slightly crouched position.

For advanced practitioners, it is also possible to perform this exercise with your legs extended.

Tips

- Your head must stay as close to your chest as possible; otherwise, it will act as a brake during the movement.
- The faster you perform the exercise, the less strength you'll need.
- The biggest mistake is to turn your head sideways and roll over one shoulder, which would be similar to a Judo roll.
- Don't push off with your hands too early; only do so when your legs are at least above your head. Otherwise, you'll push yourself back instead of in the direction of the movement.

Spotting

As a spotter, your main task is to assist with the transition from lying on the back to the squat position. To do this, you can either use both hands from one side to grip the turner's thigh and help lift them with a gentle pull, or you can position yourself behind the turner, using one hand on each thigh from underneath to provide similar assistance.

The L-Seat

Description
The L-Seat is a classic exercise in calisthenics but is also used in floor gymnastics. While supporting yourself on your hands, you lift both legs, either spread or straight, to at least horizontal level.

Preliminary Exercises
This exercise primarily requires a lot of strength and is made easier by flexibility. Therefore, it is advisable to focus on stretching the thighs and training the abdominal and arm muscles before starting these exercises.

Lifting Legs and Buttocks

Start by sitting on the floor with either your legs extended straight and together or spread apart. Place your hands on the floor at knee height and keep your back as straight as possible. Lift both legs as high as you can and repeat this exercise at least ten times. If this is too challenging at first, place both hands beside one knee and lift only that leg.

Next, place your hands beside your hips (or between your legs if your legs are spread). Push your buttocks up while keeping your feet on the floor. It is crucial that your upper body leans forward rather than backward during this movement.

Tuck L-Seat

The difficulty of the L-Seat position lies not only in the arm strength required but also in the flexibility needed to bring your legs close to your body, along with the strength to overcome gravity.

To train just the necessary arm strength, start by pulling both legs in toward your body and then pushing yourself up. If this works well, gradually decrease the bend in your legs or extend one leg at a time.

One-Leg L-Seat

Perform the L-Seat with just one leg raised in the air. Alternate between legs to build the necessary strength for each. If needed, you can use the grounded foot to apply slight pressure to the floor.

Ensure that you actively lift the extended leg upward, which may cause a stretching sensation.

Execution of the L-Seat

Straight-Leg Variant: Sit in a pike position with your legs extended straight in front of you. Place your hands on the floor beside your hips. Lean your upper body slightly forward and push yourself off the floor with your hands. Engage your abdominal muscles and thighs, actively lifting your legs upward.

Straddle Variant: Sit in a wide straddle position and place your hands on the floor between your legs. Roll back slightly, lifting your legs as you do so. If needed, you can bend your knees slightly. Roll forward again, pressing your hands firmly into the floor. Bring your chest over your hands so that your arms form a 90-degree angle with the floor, and lift your legs.

Tips
- The L-Seat is not an exercise you can master in a day—unless you already have the necessary strength and flexibility. Practice the relevant preliminary exercises daily, and at first, aim to hold the position for just a few seconds.
- It can be more motivating to practice the support hold on an elevated surface initially. This way, your legs will stay in the air even if they don't reach a horizontal position.

Spotting
Not necessary.

Techniques for Professionals

These techniques represent the pinnacle of gymnastics. While the order in which you learn them can be varied, I strongly recommend not attempting to learn the back handspring and the backward somersault simultaneously, as this often leads to confusion.

Many would say that these exercises can no longer be learned at home and require joining a gym or club. I partially agree with this.

What I cannot recommend is trying to master these techniques entirely on your own. I know plenty of teenagers who have taught themselves many of these exercises by jumping off their beds, using a backyard trampoline, or in a trampoline park without any spotting. There are some natural athletes capable of such incredible feats, but they are the exception rather than the rule.

To safely learn these techniques, you need a good, strong helper and, ideally, at least a crash mat to cushion hard falls. Handsprings, flips, and aerial cartwheels can be wonderfully and safely practiced in a trampoline park with a foam pit or airbag.

For all other techniques, I recommend working on them slowly with a helper to learn the movement patterns and then gradually increasing the speed.

The Press Handstand

Description

The press handstand is an exceptionally challenging move that requires not only technical skill but also significant strength and, ideally, flexibility. In this exercise, you place your hands on the floor and lift your legs into a handstand through a straddle position using bare strength, without jumping.

Preliminary Exercises

To master the press handstand, you need to build a significant amount of strength and flexibility. The less flexible you are, the more strength you'll need. Ideally, you should be able to lay your upper body on the floor while in a straddle position to ensure you have the necessary flexibility.

For strength training, besides practicing the handstand, I recommend push-ups where your hands are placed not vertically but closer to your hips. This position mimics the arm placement and load you'll experience during the press handstand, helping you build the specific muscle strength required for this advanced skill.

Elevated Press

Place your hands on an elevated surface, ideally at chest height. A bar, stable table, or wall can work well for this. Pull your hips up without jumping, aiming to bring your feet as close to your hands as possible. Perform the movement as slowly and controlled as possible, keeping your body tight and avoiding momentum. Slowly and carefully lower your hips back down to the starting position. Repeat this exercise multiple times to build strength and control. Maintain tension throughout your entire body, especially in your core. Breathe evenly and calmly to help control your movements, and actively stabilize your shoulders to minimize strain on your arms and wrists.

Press Handstand Against the Wall

Place your hands on the floor at a distance from the wall that feels comfortable for you. The further away your hands are from the wall, the easier the exercise will be. Spread your legs wide apart. Lean your upper back against the wall. Push down on your hands and try to press your hips against the wall, allowing your legs to follow. Once your hips are against the wall, pull your legs up into the handstand position.

This exercise is perfect for learning the movement pattern and can be adjusted in difficulty by changing the distance between your hands and the wall.

Negative Press Handstand

Get into a handstand. If you can't hold it steadily for long, perform the exercise against a wall. Spread your legs wide apart, push your shoulders forward toward your back, bend your hips, and slowly move your legs toward the ground. Ideally, only your hips and eventually your back should curl.

This exercise helps you practice the movement and strengthens the right muscles for the press handstand, making it easier since you're working with gravity rather than against it.

Press Handstand from elevation

This exercise only makes sense if you have sufficient flexibility. Stand on a slight elevation and perform the Swiss Handstand as described in the „Execution" section. After successfully completing the movement, gradually reduce the elevation each time to work your way toward the final form.

Execution of the Press Handstand

Place your hands on the ground as close to your feet as possible and spread your legs. Push your shoulders slightly towards your back. Allow your hips and lower back to follow your shoulders, so that your feet are „pulled" off the ground. Continue lifting your legs over the straddle and bring them together once they are horizontal to the floor. At the same time, push your shoulders back and straighten into a handstand.

Tips

• Proper technique is crucial to get into a handstand with minimal effort. You need maximum strength in your shoulder girdle to push your shoulders forward and hold that position.
• Make sure you don't fall into an arch. Your entire back needs to „roll up" from the shoulders.
• If you lack flexibility but have strong arms, you can slightly bend your arms during this exercise to achieve a similar effect to pushing your shoulders forward.

Spotting

The spotter replaces the wall from the initial exercise. Stand behind the gymnast. Once he has shifted his shoulders forward, support him with your knees. Grasp his thighs close to the hips and assist the upward movement with a gentle pull.

If the gymnast is more advanced, you don't need to stabilize his shoulders anymore and only support the legs.

The Flick-Flack

Description

The flick-flack or back handspring is a skill that should definitely be learned with spotting, due to the high risk of injury if not executed correctly. From a slightly crouched position, you jump backward with an arched back, landing in a handstand. You then push off with your hands and return to a normal standing position.

Preliminary Exercises

There are countless preliminary exercises for the flick-flack that help develop a feel for its execution. Since the flick-flack is a highly complex move, I recommend performing each of these exercises diligently.

Jump in soft mats

To perform this exercise optimally, you'll need at least a soft mat or a large, soft, slightly elevated surface. Alternatively, you can use a wall, ideally padded for safety. This exercise simulates the starting movement of a flick-flack.

Performing Against the Wall: Lean your back against a wall. Position your feet a little away from the wall and align your thighs horizontally to the floor. Keep your arms extended downward and forward. Simultaneously, stretch your legs and quickly pull your arms backward.

Performing on a Mat: Stand in front of your soft elevated surface. Squat down as if you were about to sit on a chair, making sure your knees do not move forward and your thighs are parallel to the floor. Your arms should be extended downward and forward, with your back straight or slightly arched (don't bow down!).

From this position, you should feel like you're about to fall backward. Instead, extend your legs forcefully, pull your arms quickly backward, and jump into a slight overextension towards your elevated surface. Your hands should make contact first, and your body should remain extended and tight.

Snapdown from Wall Handstand

Begin by kicking up into a handstand against a wall. Position your hands about two hand lengths or more away from the wall, so your back is slightly arched.

From this position, push off with your feet and pull your legs quickly toward the floor. This will give you a sense of the end phase of a flick-flack.

Ideally, you should have a spotter who supports your back and, if necessary, provides a slight initial push.

Alternatively, if you have a spotter or are very confident in your handstand, you can perform this exercise without the wall. A slight elevation can be useful here to give you more time to execute the snapdown.

Half Flick from Elevation

For this exercise, you need an elevated surface and good back flexibility. Depending on your height, this could be a bed or an elevation about the height of a table. Make sure to place a mat on the floor in front of the elevation.

Ideally, you should have one or two spotters who can support your shoulders and back to prevent landing on your head.

Lie on your back on the elevation, letting your arms hang over the edge. Slide further off the edge until your hands can touch the floor. Ideally, your torso should be nearly vertical to the ground. If you're not flexible enough, you will need a spotter to stabilize your back and provide a slight push-off.

Push off with your feet and pull your legs quickly towards the floor.

Flick-Flack from the Cradle

For this exercise, you need either a very strong spotter or two helpers standing opposite each other.

Sit with your thighs on the close spotter's forearm, while your lower back is supported by the far spotter's arm. Arch your arms and back backward, and as your spotter rotates their arms in the direction of movement, they will help you reach the floor with your hands.

The spotter will give you a gentle push with their near hand, allowing you to perform a half Flick-Flack, similar to the previous exercise.

Once you are comfortable with this exercise and your spotter feels confident, try generating the necessary push-off with your feet from the floor.

Flick-Flack Over a Roll

This exercise is especially useful if you have the right equipment at home and feel confident with the movement. Make sure you have enough mats to cushion a potential fall. Initially, having a spotter to assist or secure your equipment is recommended.

For this exercise, you can use a Flick-Flack roll, a mat rolled up to at least hip height, or a suitably large exercise ball. Note that an exercise ball may roll away to the side.

Position yourself in front of your equipment and get into the starting position for a Flick-Flack. Perform the Flick-Flack as described in „Execution." Your equipment will help ensure that your lower back is high enough and that you don't fall onto your back.

Start by performing the exercise slowly, pushing yourself up onto the equipment, reaching down with your hands to the floor, and pulling your feet down. Gradually increase the speed and use more power as you become more comfortable with the movement.

Execution of the Flick-Flack

Stand up straight with your arms raised. Your hands should be facing forward or slightly inward – never outward.

Slightly bend your knees so that they do not move forward, keep your gaze downward, and swing your arms (with your thighs as horizontal to the floor as possible).

Push off energetically with your feet and quickly swing your arms behind your ears. Arch your back and keep your core engaged.

Land in an overextended handstand position. Immediately press down with your shoulders to push off from your hands, pull your legs down, and return to a standing position.

For advanced practitioners, this exercise can be performed from a roundoff. It's crucial to pull your feet as close to your hands as possible after the roundoff and take your time to transition smoothly.

Tips

- The flick-flack is a move that often fails due to fear. Practice it as much as possible with support until you are absolutely confident that you can perform it on your own.
- To transition from a supported flick-flack to an unsupported one, it is recommended that the spotter gradually reduces their involvement by keeping their hands near the gymnast throughout the movement, ready to intervene if needed.
- It is easier to practice the flick-flack on a sloped surface, a small elevation, or a trampoline initially.
- If you have access to an air track, it is ideal for practicing the flick-flack because it provides support both during the takeoff and when pushing off with your hands.

- **Spotting**

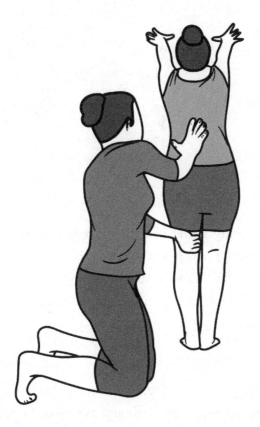

For inexperienced spotters, I recommend using two strong ones who stand opposite each other. The spotter should grasp the thigh near the knee with one hand, while the other hand supports the lower back. The first hand provides a push and helps the gymnast bring his legs quickly to the ground, while the second hand supports from below to prevent a fall.

Even though it may be challenging, the flick-flack should initially be practiced in slow motion with assistance to perfect the technique and ensure that the necessary strength is present to prevent any potential falls.

The Front Handspring

Description

The front handspring is the inverse movement of the flick-flack. It requires less courage and poses a lower risk of injury but is technically more demanding. From a run-up or hop, you swing powerfully into a handstand, push off from the shoulders, and roll over into a standing position.

Preliminary Exercises

Before attempting this exercise, it's crucial that your handstand is solid. There are countless preliminary exercises to prepare for this move. The most important aspect, in my view, is learning to push off from the shoulders, which is essential for the front handspring. Without a proper shoulder push-off, you may end up arching your back excessively, which technically resembles a bridge more than a proper handspring. The correct technique involves only a slight back arch and a highly efficient flight phase.

Handstand Hop

You can practice this exercise regularly as a supplementary drill. It might take some time to perfect it.

First, kick up into a handstand. As you push off from the push off leg, focus on pushing your shoulders. Imagine trying to push the floor or mat away with your hands. This will create a small hop. Try to remain stable in the handstand position after the hop.

Important: Avoid achieving the hop by bending your arms. Although this is possible, it requires a lot of strength and is too slow for most gymnasts. Instead, to get a feel for shoulder pressure, try leaning against a wall with your arms extended. Push off the wall without bending your arms or using your hands. Alternatively, go into a push-up position and jump up without using your back, arms, or hands – only by gently giving way in your shoulders first and then explosively pushing through them.

Handstand Falling

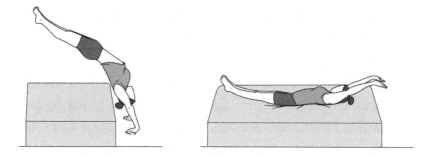

For this exercise, you definitely need a soft landing area – ideally a cushioned mat, though a mattress can also work if necessary.

Kick up into a handstand quickly, keep your gaze on your hands, slightly arch your back, and let yourself fall onto the mat while remaining tense. If you are already comfortable with handstand hops, you can combine the two exercises. Ideally, your heels should touch the ground first.

This exercise helps you overcome the fear of falling and teaches you to maintain tension in the handstand even while falling.

There are two variations of this exercise, both aiming to maintain tension in the air. In the first variation, tighten your core so that your legs stay in the air and you only land on your back (boat position). The second variation, which I find more effective but also more challenging, involves maintaining a slightly arched position where only your upper back and feet touch the ground. The second variation is more difficult but more closely resembles the landing position of the front handspring.

Foot Whips Against the Wall

This exercise primarily helps you learn to swing quickly into a handstand and bring both legs into position simultaneously. Stand in front of a padded wall (ideally with a gymnastics mat leaned against it).

Swing into a slightly arched handstand with a hand's length distance from the mat as quickly as possible. Your feet should hit the wall simultaneously, making a loud noise to indicate that you have enough momentum.

Handspring from an Elevated Platform

For this exercise, you'll ideally need a vaulting box or a similar piece of equipment. Depending on your skill level, a platform with less height may also be sufficient. Perform the front handspring as described in the „Execution" section, starting from the elevated surface with your hands placed on it.

One or two spotters may be necessary, especially for higher platforms, as there's a risk of over-rotating and landing on your face. Therefore, I recommend landing on the softest possible surface to minimize the risk of injury.

This exercise is particularly useful if your Handstand Hop isn't yet strong enough to achieve the necessary height.

Front Handspring on an Elevated Surface

A soft mat or two stacked mattresses work well for this exercise. Perform the front handspring with a hop or a run-up, placing your hands on the elevated surface. The altered angle of your arms relative to the platform makes it easier to push off, helping you complete the front handspring more successfully.

An alternative method I often let my gymnasts practice before attempting the handspring on a standard mat is to place their hands in front of the elevated surface. This means the handspring will only succeed if the push-off from the shoulders is exceptionally strong. For this variation, a spotter should be positioned next to the gymnast to catch them if they fall backward into a supine position.

Once this exercise is successfully performed, the handspring on a regular mat should usually be achievable without additional aids.

Execution of the front handspring

From a standing position or a short run-up, perform a broad, flat hop into a split stance and swing your arms overhead. Place your hands next to each other on the ground. You need to push away from the push off leg with much more energy than for a normal handstand, while also swinging the lead leg. Before reaching vertical, your push off leg should catch up with your lead leg.

Immediately after pushing off with the push off leg, push away from the shoulders so that your hands lift off the ground. Look towards your hands, slightly arch your back, and keep your body tight. Land on one or both legs while maintaining your gaze towards your hands.

Tips

- Reach forward as much as possible to ensure your shoulders are fully opened; otherwise, you're more likely to end up in a rolling motion.
- Practice the handspring from an elevated surface initially and gradually decrease the height.
- If you have an airtrack, it's ideal for providing extra height, though landing on it can be more challenging.

Spotting

For this exercise, having two spotters is definitely beneficial, but a single strong one usually suffices.

Your role is to ensure the gymnast doesn't land on his back. The hand closest to the gymnast should grasp the upper back, while the other hand supports the lower back. Stabilize the movement and push up gently after the landing if necessary to prevent the gymnast from tipping back. If needed, you can also lift the gymnast slightly with both hands to help them feel how much they need to push off to achieve the optimal height.

The Forward Somersault

Description

The forward somersault is typically performed from a running start, during which you complete a full rotation in the air and then land back on your feet. Although it is technically more challenging than the backward somersault, I recommend learning it first because it tends to be less intimidating and you already have a basic understanding of the movement from learning the forward roll.

Learning the somersault safely requires a lot of equipment and experience for proper spotting. Therefore, it's best to practice the somersault initially in a trampoline park with a foam pit to prevent injuries.

Preliminary Exercises

To perform a somersault, you need two essential things: a lot of jumping power and strong abdominal muscles. You must be able to roll up and extend quickly.

Roll Up on the Ground

This is a very simple exercise that helps you learn the most crucial part of the somersault „dry.“

Lie on your back with your arms extended overhead. Pull your feet in and fold your torso quickly towards your thighs. Your hands should grab your shins. Just as quickly, return to the extended position.

It's important to feel like you're righting yourself. Your movement impulse should go forward toward your feet.

Running Jump

Take three to four steps of a run-up, jump off one leg as flat and far as possible, and bring your arms into a high position. Land on the balls of both feet and spring off, without letting your heels touch the ground.

It is crucial that your arms reach the high position with the takeoff and not only during the bounce, as this would create a counter-movement to the somersault.

Ensure that you lift your arms only up to ear level and not beyond. It's better to keep your arms at a moderate height and maintain a straight torso rather than falling into a hollow back due to excessive swinging.

Roll on Elevated Surface

This exercise is one of my personal favorites for learning the somersault, but it requires the right equipment.

You'll need an elevated surface, ideally a springboard long enough to roll over. Ensure the area behind the elevation is cushioned, preferably with a soft mat.

Start with a run-up, jump off both legs, and perform a roll over the elevated surface, ending with your feet extending over the edge and landing back on your feet. Ideally, have one or two helpers to prevent you from falling sideways or to catch you if you grab the surface too far back and fall during the roll.

Once you're comfortable with this, you can try placing your hands on the surface only during the flight phase, or if you're using a very soft elevation, attempt to land directly in a squat on the elevated surface without putting your hands down. The goal is to transition from landing in a squat with the elevation to landing standing up without it.

Somersault with Shoulder Support

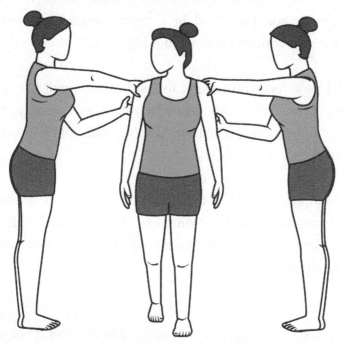

This exercise is highly recommended if the previous one is not feasible for you. It's also very helpful for overcoming the fear of performing a somersault, which is often the biggest obstacle.

You'll need two strong helpers to support you. Position them on either side of you: one helper should place their near hand on your upper arm from the front and their far hand on your shoulder from above. Jump and perform a somersault in the air without pulling your arms. Your helpers will guide and support you through the motion, with the far hand providing stability to prevent you from falling.

The goal of this exercise is to rely as little as possible on the far hand, aiming to complete the somersault quickly and efficiently.

Once you're comfortable with this, you can try performing the exercise from a run-up. Just remember not to raise your arms during the jump.

Execution of the forward somersault

Take three to four steps to build momentum, then jump off one leg as far and flat as possible. Land in a slight forward lean with your hands raised but without bending your hips.

Spring off your feet with a slight forward motion, pull your legs up, and bring your upper body towards your legs. Move your arms vigorously downward. To achieve a tighter position, you can grasp your lower legs.

As you complete about three-quarters of the rotation, extend your body and prepare to land on your feet. Slightly bend your legs to absorb the landing, but avoid sinking deeper than a horizontal position with your thighs.

Tips

- The most common mistake in a forward somersault is not jumping high enough. To address this, start by performing the somersault on a soft, elevated surface so you land in a squat position, and then gradually reduce the height of the elevation.
- It is crucial to jump with a flat trajectory to effectively transfer the forward momentum from your run into the jump.
- Try not to look down when jumping, as this can cause you to jump lower than intended.

Spotting

For a forward somersault, I recommend using two spotters, especially if you lack experience. The standard spotting technique involves the sandwich grip. This technique requires the spotters to position their hands opposite the direction of the somersault's rotation. One spotter places their far hand on the gymnast's back and their near hand on the gymnast's abdomen. This grip allows the spotters to help rotate the gymnast in the air and catch them if something unexpected occurs.

A slightly safer but potentially uncomfortable variation for the gymnast involves placing the far hand on the gymnast's shoulder from above. This method allows the spotter to lift the gymnast if necessary. The downside is that if the somersault is too low, the pressure on the shoulder can be uncomfortable, and it can also make it more challenging for the spotters to assist with the rotation.

The backward somersault

Description

The back somersault can be performed both from a standing position and from a roundoff. After a powerful jump backward, you rotate in the air and complete a full turn around your body's axis before landing back on your feet.

I strongly recommend practicing the back somersault with extensive assistance and initially using a foam pit in a trampoline gym, as mistakes can result in serious injuries.

Preliminary Exercises

For the back somersault, you should already have the necessary conditioning skills from performing the forward somersault. Your jumping power is also crucial here.

Roll up on the Floor

Similar to the forward somersault, you can practice the rolling motion for the back somersault on the floor. Lie on your back, extend your arms and legs, and quickly pull your knees towards your head while keeping your upper body slightly raised. It's best not to pull your arms towards your legs, as this would create a counterproductive movement.

Instead, move your arms in a sideways motion towards your legs.

Backward Roll Over a Elevated Surface

You can perform this exercise similarly to the forward somersault if you have a suitable elevated surface. Jump backward onto the elevation, roll backwards so that your hands make contact with the edge of the surface, and land with your feet on the floor behind it. Initially, it's perfectly fine – and safer – to use a larger elevation and complete the backward roll entirely on it.

As a final exercise, you can try to complete the roll in the air and land in a squat position.

It's highly recommended to have a spotter to catch or slow you down in case you land too far forward or backward on the elevation.

Backward Jump with Assistance

This exercise is essential for learning the backward somersault and is particularly effective on a springy surface like a mini-trampoline or airtrack.

Perform a backward jump from with swinging your arms from a horizontal position into a high lift. Your helper will hold your hips or upper back. Aim to gain height with your jump and push against your partner. Your partner will push you back so you land in the same spot from where you jumped.

Next, tuck your legs in. Mentally, imagine you are aiming to land on an elevated surface. Ideally, you will manage to briefly land almost horizontally with your legs tucked on your partner's hands.

Shoulder Somersault

For this exercise, you'll need a strong partner and a soft landing area, as you're likely to fall onto your back at some point. This exercise is particularly useful if you have the technical skills but lack the courage to perform the backward somersault on your own.

Jump similarly to the „Backward Jump with Assistance" exercise. Your partner should be strong and ideally positioned on his knees or slightly crouched, depending on your size relative to them. If needed, your partner should spread his legs behind him to prevent you from landing on his legs.

Jump backward, tuck your legs, and this time, instead of pushing you back, your partner will lightly lift you upward. He should roll you over their shoulder by turning his head to the side. As you roll over his shoulder, extend your legs and prepare to land on your feet.

Execution of the Backward Somersault

From a Stand: Bend your knees slightly, swing your arms down and back, and jump by explosively extending your legs.

From a Trampoline: Bounce once or twice to gain momentum, then spring off with a powerful push.

From a roundoff: Land with your feet a bit farther from your hands, avoid touching the ground with your heels, and immediately push off the ground with a powerful bounce.

Pull your hands up to your head but not beyond your ears. At the same time, tuck your legs towards your torso. If you're not being spotted, pull your arms down towards your shins over the side. Otherwise, you can keep them in a high position.

After a three-quarter turn, extend your legs and land, slightly bending your knees. Your thighs should ideally drop no lower than horizontal.

Tips

- The backward somersault is a fear-based skill. Therefore, use spotting for as long as needed until you feel completely confident.
- The easiest way to practice the somersault is on a trampoline with preliminary jumps. Learning it from a roundoff is more suited for club sports with skilled helpers.
- A common mistake is tilting the head back. This reduces height, makes it harder to tuck in, and often results in landing on your knees. You can avoid this by placing a pair of socks or similar between your chin and chest.

Spotting

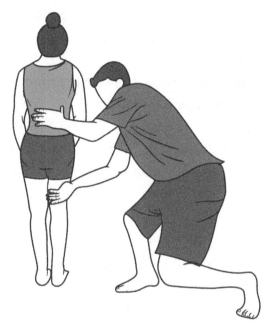

For this exercise, it's beneficial to have two spotters standing opposite each other.

With one hand, grip the thigh close to the knee and provide the gymnast with a push to help him rotate quickly.

With the other hand, support the lower back to provide a rotational axis and help the gymnast gain the necessary height.

Your hands should move with the gymnast. Initially, you should actively support the exercise. If you have appropriate equipment (such as a soft landing mat), you can gradually try to reduce the push with one hand.

Once the backward somersault is going well, I usually only hold the back with one hand, keeping the other hand at a slight distance to provide additional push if needed.

The Aerial

Description

The aerial, or free cartwheel, is a powerful, high-flying cartwheel performed without hand contact with the ground. Unlike a regular cartwheel, it is crucial to bring the legs back to the ground as quickly as possible, which is why the Aerial is usually executed with a short, compact movement rather than a wide one. This technique is particularly challenging for taller individuals and requires extensive practice.

Preliminary Exercises

The basic preparatory exercise for the Aerial is a fast cartwheel. You should aim to perform your cartwheel as quickly as possible, so you can easily execute a one-armed cartwheel with the opposite hand. Additionally, mastering the straddle split significantly simplifies the movement. To actively pull up your legs, practice pulling the straddle split while jumping or, if you are seated in the straddle split, tightening your thigh muscles and slightly lifting your feet off the ground.

Aerial from an Elevated Surface

The easiest exercise to get accustomed to performing a cartwheel without using your hands is to practice the free cartwheel from an elevated surface. Start by practicing a regular cartwheel from the elevation, then move on to a one-armed cartwheel (using the opposite hand), and finally, try to lift your hands off the ground while performing the cartwheel. It's important to execute the cartwheel very quickly and ensure that your swinging leg lands back on the ground as soon as possible.

Aerial Over an Elevated Surface

For this exercise, you will need either a helper as described in „Spotting" or a jumping aid. A trampoline or an airtrack, along with an elevation of 1-2 soft landing mats, works well for this.

Perform a strong jump from the trampoline or with the assistance of your partner to complete a cartwheel, placing your hands on the elevated surface and landing with your feet behind it. When jumping off a trampoline, your movement might resemble a roundoff more, as you are likely to jump off with both feet simultaneously.

If you achieve enough height, attempt to perform the cartwheel over the elevation without touching it with your hands or only touching it briefly at the last moment. If successful, try pulling your hands upward as described under „Execution."

Execution of the Aerial

From a running start with a hop, extend your push off leg forward and push yourself powerfully upward. Your front arm moves in the direction of a regular cartwheel but is pulled up past the ground to generate momentum. Your rear arm follows this movement upward.

Your lead leg should be pushed upward as quickly as possible. The wider you spread your legs, the better. Actively pull your lead leg downwards so you can quickly return to your feet. Follow this by pulling up your push off leg.

Tips

- Before attempting an Aerial, ensure that your cartwheel is fast enough that you barely need to use your hands.
- Regularly stretch your splits to increase your leg span, which reduces the height you need.
- Initially, you might not lift your arms due to fear. Practice the final form as often as possible with spotting, so you can get used to the idea that your hands won't touch the ground even if you extend them.

Spotting

As a spotter, position yourself on the side where the gymnast places his push off leg. Ideally, practice a few times dry to determine where you need to stand to be in the right position immediately after the jump. Otherwise, move towards the gymnast so that you are directly next to him as he begins the exercise.

Place your hands on top of each other and bend your arms. With both hands, grasp the gymnast's hips from the front.
Actively push him upwards to provide additional height and a rotational axis.
It is also possible to secure the gymnast with a type of rotational grip (see Forward Somersault). This can be helpful if the aerial is being performed slowly due to fear and you want to maintain maximum control as a spotter or help the gymnast overcome his fear. The drawback is that this method can sometimes slow down or hinder the execution of the move.

The Back Walkover

Description
The back walkover, regardless of the direction, requires immense flexibility and is definitely not suitable for every gymnast.

From a standing position, lift one leg straight up, arch your back backward until you place your hands on the floor, pass through a handstand position with a split in the air, and land in a lunge position.

Preliminary Exercises
With the right flexibility, the back walkover can theoretically be learned completely without spotting. However, it greatly accelerates the learning process if you can perform the final exercise with assistance earlier.

When stretching for this exercise, the bridge is especially important. You should try to bring your hands and feet as close together as possible in the bridge position. Additionally, it's essential to train the split.

Bridge from a Standing Position

For this exercise, I recommend using a wall behind you, a mat under your body, and/or a spotter to support your back.

Stand upright, stretch your arms overhead, and look at your hands. Reach your arms further back while simultaneously arching your back. Ensure you are bending your entire back, not just the lower part. Your knees will likely move slightly forward to balance the weight.

Touch the wall with your hands and walk down it until you land in the bridge position.

As you improve, you can take larger steps on the wall or reach the wall later in the process.

Kick Over

Once you master this exercise, you will have everything you need for the walkover.

Get into the bridge position. Straighten your legs so that your shoulders are fully stretched. Lift one leg straight up (it might be easier at first to lift it bent).

With the other leg, push off the ground and pull the upper leg back, so you come through a brief handstand into a standing position.

A spotter can assist you by initially holding your upper leg and giving you additional lift. Additionally, you can perform the bridge with elevated legs to shorten the distance you need to cover.

Execution of the back walkover

Stand upright. Move your arms straight over your head, and follow your hands with your gaze. At the same time, lift one leg straight up. As your arms reach vertical, arch your back, allowing your arms to stretch as far back as possible.

Your lifted leg should follow this movement. Once you make contact with the ground using your hands, push off with your back leg. Briefly enter a handstand with your legs in a split and then pull your front leg as close as possible to your hands on the ground. The other leg will follow, landing in a step position.

Tips

- The back walkover is a flexibility exercise. It can theoretically be performed with a jump, but this reduces its elegance and places a high strain on your spine.
- The bridge is the fundamental element for this exercise. However, it's crucial to focus on increase shoulder flexibility, rather than just making your lower back more flexible.
- An airtrack can make this exercise easier by providing more momentum during the push-off from the back leg, helping you get past the handstand. Ideally, in the final form, this should be achieved without additional momentum.

Spotting

As a spotter, stand next to the gymnast on the side where he is lifting his leg. If there are two spotters, they should stand on either side of the gymnast, with the one on the „wrong" side only supporting the back.

With your hand farthest from the gymnast, grasp his leg just above the knee bend, and with the other hand, support their lower back.

The far hand provides propulsion and assists with the movement, while the near hand supports from underneath to prevent a fall.

Once the back handspring is performed well enough, you can gradually remove the hand that supports the momentum.

The Front Walkover

Description

In a front walkover, you start in a handstand with a split, tilt towards your back, and land on one leg.

Although the front walkover might feel easier in principle, I recommend practicing the backward version first. Many gymnasts train this move by simply letting themselves fall, which often leads to excessive stretching of the lower back and can cause long-term spinal damage.

Preliminary exercises

The most important preparatory exercise for this movement is the back walkover. Once you have mastered this, you have the necessary skills to tackle the forward version as well. Additionally, you should be able to balance well in a handstand for the front walkover.

In theory, you could perform the front walkover against a wall and complete the downward movement by climbing down. However, in practice, it's much more effective to learn the exercise through spotting and regular repetition.

Execution of the front walkover

Swing into a handstand, and instead of extending both legs straight into the air, balance your position by stretching one leg toward your back and the other toward your stomach (split). Overextend your shoulders and upper back so that your body forms a „C" shape. Then, gently bend your lower back while keeping your abs engaged to control the forward leg as it descends toward the ground. It is crucial to place this leg as close to your hands as possible. Actively push the back leg forward to land in a lunge position.

Tips

- Placing the first leg close to your hands is crucial for landing smoothly in the lunge position. If you fall during this exercise, this is usually the issue.
- Initially, you can practice the front walkover with a bit of momentum to get accustomed to the transition.
- If you're unable to position your leg close enough to your hands to lift yourself back up independently, continue stretching your bridge and try to bring your feet and hands closer together.

Spotting

As a spotter, position yourself beside the gymnast. Once the gymnast goes into a handstand, use your nearest hand to hold the upper back and your far hand to support the lower back.

The nearest hand helps extend the shoulders by applying pressure in that direction. Additionally, you lift the gymnast into the air after the leg placement.

The far hand provides gentle counterpressure to control the lowering of the first leg and prevent abrupt falling during this transition. If back flexibility is not an issue, support can also be provided at the arm (see illustration).

Acknowledgments

My first thanks go to the many readers of my first books. The success of my initial book motivated me to embark on another project of this kind and finally the success of the german version to translate it in english.

The second major thank you goes to the many diligent acrobats who attend my classes. Through the diverse experiences I have had as a trainer, I gained the understanding of what it takes to learn a technique. Often, I encountered students for whom my previous repertoire of preliminary exercises was insufficient, prompting me to continually research and experiment with how I could improve my approach.

Of course, not everything I do in training is included in this book, as the material requirements would be too great for personal use. However, I have adapted many preliminary exercises so that they are feasible for many individuals practicing at home.

Thank you for dedicating your attention to floor gymnastics and thereby helping to ensure that humans do not completely forget how to move aesthetically. If you have feedback on the book, I thank you in advance, as it will help me tailor it perfectly to the needs of my readers.

Conclusion

Whenever I lie at the swimming pool, in the park, or on the beach, or perhaps practice gymnastics myself, I always smile when I see a young child doing cartwheels or attempting a handstand.

I hope that this book contributes to seeing more of such moments. In our increasingly sedentary world, I sometimes feel that for some people, the development of movement skills stops at simply walking on two legs.

Especially in urban areas, where I worked as a gymnastics teacher, I encountered children who even struggled to hop on one leg. Our children are not to blame for their lack of agility. They either lack opportunities or are held back by very cautious adults.

I fully understand concerns about planning for your child to perform somersaults. However, at least the basic techniques of gymnastics should be considered achievable for every child. And when parents actively participate, it also strengthens family bonds and mutual trust.

And who knows, maybe even some adults, over the age of thirty, will find the motivation to learn the handstand once again?

I hope you enjoyed reading this book and found joy in learning as many of these exercises as possible.

Sebastian

Made in the USA
Las Vegas, NV
27 November 2024

12767779R00085